- Successful Dating -

No More Frogs
Libra

23 September – 22 October

by
Cathrine Dahl

CONTENTS

- Successful Dating -
No More Frogs

by Cathrine Dahl

No More Frogs - Successful Dating is your one-stop dating guide. No unnecessary blah-blah. The information is right here, at your fingertips.

This guide can be used in several ways. It's a handy tool when you want to prepare yourself a little. It can give you an advantage when going on a date or getting to know someone you've just met - or even someone you've known for a while.

Although this guide can help you angle your approach, remember to be true to yourself. Have fun, be wise, follow your heart - and keep your feet on the ground!

- Cathrine Dahl

Preface:
A few words about compatibility, and why compatibility guides can give you the wrong idea.

So you've met this Gemini you really, really like, but you're a Scorpio, and the compatibility guides say you're a lousy match. Guess what? That's rubbish!

Some compatibility guides offer a very simplistic approach, claiming that your best matches are the star signs within the same element as you:

Fire: Aries, Leo and Sagittarius
Earth: Taurus, Virgo and Capricorn
Air: Gemini, Libra and Aquarius
Water: Cancer, Scorpio and Pisces

Other guides are slightly more specific, declaring that we are compatible with star signs within our astrological polarity.

Yin: Taurus, Virgo, Capricorn, Cancer, Scorpio and Pisces
Yang: Aries, Leo, Sagittarius, Gemini, Libra and Aquarius

Doesn't look too good, does it? The most optimistic approach has removed half of the population from your dating pool. It doesn't make any sense. The true picture is far more promising...

One star sign, two very different personalities

Each of us has a unique astrological thumbprint determined by the sun, the moon and the planets. The most important factors being your ascending star (ascendant), the sun (star sign) and the moon (feelings).

Let's make it simple

Imagine your star sign being a melody. All the other aspects (the unique positioning of the moon and the planets) are sound effects, applied by a producer with a mixer.

The combination of rhythm, depth and base creates your unique sound. Another person with the same star sign will get his own sound mix and end up with a different beat.

Your personal melody can create wonderful harmonies with star signs you're not supposed to get on with – and nothing but noise with signs that are meant to be matches. You won't find out until you get to know each other.

Let's get to know your date...

THE MALE

YOUR DATE: LIBRA
23 September–22 October

The Essence of him

Artistic – creative – kind – diplomatic – restless – charming – genuine – has a strong sense of justice – a lover of beauty – compassionate – fond of people – a romantic drifter – intelligent – indecisive – has a strong work ethic – inclusive – big-hearted – polite – optimistic – attentive – sensual –stands up for people who are not able to do so themselves

...and remember: Aesthetics are important to him, and this applies to every facet of his life. Crudeness, vulgarity and insensitivity provoke him and put him off.

Blind Date – speedy essentials

Who's waiting for you?

Chances are you won't notice him right away – probably because he's already chatting away with another guest or the bartender, and they look like they've known each other for ages. There is something calm and attractive about the Libra man. His attitude and personality appear balanced and relaxed. These guys are seldom big, muscular athletes, but they carry themselves with a gentle masculinity that is very attractive. He will greet you with a warm smile and meet your eyes. Don't worry if you're a bit shy at first. This man will always give you a chance to show your true colours.

Emergency fixes for embarrassing pauses

If you feel the pauses are becoming longer, he could be testing you. Libra men have limited patience for women who have turned off their brains – no matter how beautiful they might be. Take the initiative. Impress him with something he doesn't expect you to know anything about. But make it books – not gossip magazines. Talk exotic music trends – not the latest updates on Twitter.

Your place or mine?

His attitude is calm, collected, polite and charming, but don't be fooled. Behind this distinguished exterior hides a passionate man with a healthy appetite for sex. An overnight on the first date is definitely an option if the two of you hit it off. But if you come on too strong, he might lose interest. For him, no chase means no challenge.

Checklist, before you dash out to meet him:
Tidy yourself up (hair, hands, and eyebrows)
(hint: he'll notice)
Be well rested, with no other engagements
(hint: it might get late)
Be relaxed, with smile in your eyes
(hint: dazzle him)
Wear a feminine and slightly suggestive outfit
(hint: nothing overly sexy)
Brush up on your knowledge of various topics
(hint: inspire him)

Tip: He has a jealous streak. Don't test his interest in you by flirting with other men. It'll have the opposite effect.

CHAPTER 1

PREPARE YOURSELF

Catch his eye, capture his attention
Top 10 attention grabbers

1. Be outgoing, social and cheerful.
2. Be classy. Pay attention to your manners.
3. Show interest in him by asking questions.
4. Avoid eye-popping outfits, even if they are fashionable.
5. Pay attention to your looks, and be carefully groomed from head to toe.
6. Flirt, but be discreet about it. Make him wonder...
7. Emphasise positivity in your views.
8. Show appreciation for people who succeed.
9. Pay him intelligent compliments.
10. Listen and be compassionate.

The SHE. The woman!

As with everything else in his life, his dream woman must inspire him and light up his days with beauty and positivity. He needs more than just a pretty face; inner beauty is very important to him. She must be genuine and interesting, demonstrating joy, positivity, softness and femininity combined with intelligence and independence. These are the characteristics of a real woman – according to him. And it takes a 'real woman' to keep him hooked.

The Essence of her

Feminine – intelligent – attentive – articulate – sensual and passionate – sensible – well-informed and up-to-date about current affairs – interesting, with an independent mind – encouraging and supportive – takes care of herself and her looks – outgoing and friendly in social settings – genuine – compassionate – positive– has an eye for details and the beauty in life

Libra arousal meter

From 0 to 100... In 30 minutes. He enjoys taking his time and exploring sensations – and his partner – before getting truly passionate.

Remember: Be true to yourself

It doesn't matter if he is the most stunning guy you've ever met – if you don't match, you don't match. You may be able to put on a show for a while to hold his attention, but what's the point? We can't please everybody. We all have different needs, dreams, tastes and preferences. There's no such thing as a one-size-fits-all lover. Be yourself, and be true to who you are – always!

Very important: If you want to pay him a compliment, make sure it's sincere and slightly out of the ordinary. Pay attention to details.

CHAPTER 2

THE FIRST DATE

Getting your foot in the door
The basics

A catch - and a challenge! It's much easier to capture this guy than to hold onto him. If you want him to hang around for a while – or to establish a more committed relationship – you'll need to start building a solid foundation right away.

Loves women. He may seem fascinated by you, but that doesn't guarantee he'll be there tomorrow. His interest may be genuine, but let's face it: this guy is fascinated by women in general. It takes a special someone to keep him around.

Find the right balance. Take the initiative, but be subtle about it. If you're too assertive, you'll risk pushing him away.

Aesthetics - and inner beauty. Appearance is important. He appreciates the beautiful things in life – and that includes women. You don't have to be a model. What's important is being able to radiate your inner beauty.

Eye contact is crucial. It's actually possible to seduce this guy with only your eyes. This doesn't mean you should stare him down, but playful glances and subtle nonverbal communication will go a long way.

Whatever you do...

- **DON'T** be crude or use rough language.

- **DON'T** gossip or talk negatively about other people.

- **DON'T** come on too strong.

- **DON'T** rely on your looks alone to win him over.

- **DON'T** be aggressive in your views of the world.

Remember,
Never take his interest in you for granted. If you get too comfortable and stop making

- **DON'T** pay him cheap compliments. Be observant about it.

- **DON'T** talk about former lovers or previous erotic experiences.

- **DON'T** be loud and dominate the conversation.

- **DON'T** be insensitive.

- **DON'T** flirt with other men.

an effort, it may change his perception of you.

Signs you're in - or not

It's not easy to tell with a Libra man, because he doesn't want to hurt your feelings. He could be polite, friendly and forthcoming ... but after that, he's just as likely to fade out as he is to call you. Is he staying or going? You'll have to give it a few days. It won't hurt to be assertive through a text message, but do it seductively and in a feminine way. Make sure you don't come across as aggressive. Yes, he may need a gentle nudge at times, but be careful not to nudge him out of your life. There will be obvious signs that you've captured his interest:

Chances are he will...

- return your calls immediately
- invite you out or to his home – just the two of you!
- be very attentive to your needs in bed
- ask for your opinion about things that are important to him
- include you in his plans
- act romantic and amorous

Not your type? Making an exit

Chances are that Mr. Libra will have taken off long before you start thinking about ways to call it off. He is a drifter, a dreamer and in a constant search for beauty. Combine this with a healthy appetite for the hunt, and you have someone who won't stick around for long if things aren't working out. He sees life as too precious to be wasted on a fling that's leading nowhere. And he has a big circle of friends who are

are more than happy to introduce new opportunities into his life.

However, there is always an exception to the rule: this is the Libra guy who stays around, hoping it might work out and thinking that you're just having a bad day or a bad week ... or a bad month. It's rare, but if you have dazzled him, it could happen. Don't let guilt stand in the way of happiness – for both of you. Put your foot down.

Foolproof exit measures:

If these measures don't work, you've probably got his star sign wrong. They may seem a little over the top, but for a Libra, they're sure to do the trick.

- Act like a drama queen with daily mood swings
- Tell him to speed up while having sex
- Ask him why spends so much time thinking: how about some action?
- Introduce him to some of your loud, athletic male friends (even if you have to borrow some vague acquaintances for the occasion)
- Tell him you are reinventing yourself and start wearing tacky clothes
- End every sentence with 'duh' or 'whatever'

CHAPTER 3

SEX'N STUFF

Seductive moves:
How to get him in the mood:

The Libra is one of the most aesthetic guys in the zodiac. His life is ruled by beauty and harmony – and this extends to any erotic encounter. He will respond positively to setting the mood: candles, soft pillows, a faint exotic scent, a glass of Champagne... you get the idea. He is attracted to women who manage to be passionate without appearing vulgar, and he values softness and femininity.

Preferences and erotic nature

He may sometimes need a firm and guiding partner to get him started, but as soon as his erotic feelings are lit, he will do virtually anything to please you. The only thing he won't do is rush things. He enjoys taking his time, fully exploring his partner's body and his own sensations, and giving and receiving gentle touches. This may not sound particularly passionate to you, but his soft sensuality can drive any woman wild with desire. Besides, he's no innocent little boy, and he may be open to frisky suggestions – provided they are not too crude or vulgar.

Hitting the right buttons

Although every sign has areas that are more sensitive than others, individual sensitivity may vary quite a bit. Don't go body-blind. Honing in on these erogenous zones and forgetting the rest of him is not a good idea. Use his erogenous zones to create sparks while turning him on, and as a passion booster when it gets heated. Watch his body language – including the most obvious of signs! Open your mind to the sensuality of touch and taste.

Key areas
Lower back and the buttocks

Get it on

The lower back and his buttocks are the key areas for this guy – and they're conveniently located, as they give you ample opportunity to stimulate him in public as well. Walking with your arms around each other's waists will provide an easy way to get him going - and make him want to pick up the pace in order to get back home as quickly as possible.

Arouse him

Start off by giving him an innocent massage. He loves having his bum massaged, both lightly and more deeply. If you really want him to groan with passion, you can start biting, licking and sucking his bum while gently scratching his lower back with your fingernails. Be prepared for some wild desire...

Surprise him

He gets a kick out of doing innocent things he's not supposed to do, like looking at you while you're getting undressed. Make this easy for him: leave the door slightly ajar and sensually apply lotion to your naked body – pretending you don't know he's secretly watching you.

Spice it up

Watching and being watched is a big turn-on for this guy. Suggest taking turns pleasing each other. Don't rush it. Take your time and make it sensual.

Remember: Although he may take a little while to get started, this man can go all night. Guide him gently.

His expectations

Blissful pleasure. No need to worry if you don't feel super energetic. Sometimes, it's pure bliss to lie back and enjoy being stimulated. Mr Libra doesn't mind spoiling you with sensual pleasures – provided you don't start getting lazy in bed.

Soft and sassy. His ideal partner will be feminine in bed, but he doesn't mind a little creativity.

Be original. He welcomes original ideas and suggestions, as long as they're not crude or vulgar.

Take your time. He expects his partner to appreciate the sensual and gentle nuances of sex and not to rush things. Taking time to explore and enjoy is very important to him. Orgasm chasers won't be invited back in to his bed. He loves lengthy foreplay and slowly building intense passion and pleasure.

Be present, embrace the moment. Slow caresses and gentle touches are essential for intimacy with this man.

.

Your sensual preferences
Quiz yourself and find out whether this man is for you.

Where on the scale are you?
1 = Don't agree | 3 = Sure | 5 = Agree!

1. Touch, taste and smell is very important during sex.
One a scale for 1 to 5, you are: 1 - 2 - 3- 4 - 5

2. Taking it slow is the best way to fully experience erotic pleasure.
One a scale for 1 to 5, you are: 1 - 2 - 3- 4 - 5

3. Watching each other experience pleasure can be arousing and satisfying.
One a scale for 1 to 5, you are: 1 - 2 - 3- 4 - 5

4. Vulgar language and smutty sex toys etc, can ruin the sensual pleasures of sex.
One a scale for 1 to 5, you are: 1 - 2 - 3- 4 - 5

Score 15–20: Excellent! With this kind of harmony, your erotic interactions will be intense and fulfilling.
Score 10–14: You may be able to strike the perfect balance between giving and taking. Feel free to be creative and take the initiative.
Score 5–9: Resist the urge to rush. Enjoy the slower sensual pleasures, and you may discover new erotic horizons.
Score 1–4: Allow yourself to experience sex using all your senses. This will help you enjoy every moment, not just the climax.

CHAPTER 4

GENERAL STUFF

The big picture

Keep in mind that the characteristics of a Libra may vary quite a bit depending on where within the sign he was born, as well as a wide range of additional astrological factors. But for now, let's stick to the basics. Just remember: don't jump to conclusions as soon as you meet him. Give him room to shine. Get to know the man behind the sign.

His personality: Pros and cons

Pros	Cons
• Compassionate	• Indecisive
• Intelligent	• Restless
• Romantic	• Temperamental
• Sensitive	• Commitment-avoidant
• Sensual	• Possessive
• Polite and gallant	• Jealous
• Generous	• Evasive
• Intuitive	• Falls easily in and out of love
• Diplomatic	• Insensitive when busy
• Enthusiastic	• Builds castles in the sky
• Social	• Emotionally detached
• An excellent host	• Avoidant of personal conflicts
• Has a strong work ethic	• Impractical
• Has a strong sense of justice	• Moody

Tip: How to show romantic interest

Interestingly enough, the initiative for romance usually comes from Mr. Libra. He is not particularly shy, and if you have managed to spark his interest, he won't waste any time before taking it further. At this point, all you have to do is play along.

Romantic Vibes

Mr Libra:
The dreamy and restless partner

The essence

Never take anything for granted. The Libra man loves women, and it's a lot easier to catch him than to hold onto him. Be on your toes and make an effort.

Embraces beauty. He's not really a womanizer – he just appreciates beauty and the sensuous side of life. Combine this with his indecision, and you get a guy whose interest will only be captured by someone very special.

A dreamer. He is always searching for the perfect love. This is what causes him to avoid casually entering into committed relationships.

The complete package. A stunning beauty will always be a great hit, but only for so long. Although he may feel proud to be seen with her, he won't be bothered with someone who cannot inspire him.

Clever and inspiring. A feminine and creative woman who makes him think stands the best chance of holding onto him. This may seem like hard work at times, but Mr Libra is worth it.

The big prize: He is a romantic, attentive and sensitive partner who will do his utmost to make life wonderful for his woman.

Tip: How to show erotic interest

This man is a master when it comes to observing people. He picks up on moods very quickly. Take advantage of this by focusing on sensual feelings, and communicating with your eyes. As soon as he becomes curious, add some suggestive body language.

Erotic Vibrations

Mr Libra:
The gentle and attentive lover

The essence

Passion and determination. Although he may come across as a polite gentleman, this is a very passionate guy who wants to make his partner happy - even if it takes all night.

The chase. Sex is important to a Libra – and so is the chase. Sometimes, the chase becomes the most important element, and he may lose interest if the woman doesn't live up to his expectations once he's caught her.

Sensual sixth sense. He is a determined lover who seems to know exactly what you want and when. Sometimes he may come across as a mind reader.

No need to fake it. Don't suggest anything kinky, which is not really your thing, simply because you think *he may* like it. He'll probably just smile at you and start pleasing *you* in the way he knows you want to be pleased.

Take it easy. He needs to move at his own pace. Remember not to push him.

A firm nudge! His indecisive personality may mean that you sometimes have to make decisions for him – like whether and when to make love, the bedroom or the bathroom, and so on. But these are details. Overall, this guy is an erotic dream.

CHAPTER 5

COMPATIBILITY QUIZ

Are you banging your head against the wall, or does he unleash your positive potential? Do you provoke him or bring out the best in him? Does he make you throw your arms up in exasperation, or do you feel inspired and complete in his company? Are the two of you headed towards doom or dream? Take the test to find out.

Question 1.
How do you feel about long, sensual foreplay?

A. Love it. It's a wonderful way to build up to climax.
B. Not my thing. Drawn-out foreplay tends to make me restless and impatient.
C. It's nice, provided it doesn't ruin the passion and creativity!

Question 2.
Once upon a time, there was a lonely prince... How would you continue this story?

A. There are no princes, only frogs!
B. ...who finally found his princess, and they lived happily ever after.
C. ...who turned out to be just a charming Casanova.

(cont.)

Question 3.
Do you expect your partner to express his thoughts and feelings clearly?

A. Well, he doesn't have to spell it out, provided we both understand each other.
B. Not really. His feelings can be conveyed through expressions and body language.
C. Yes. An introverted enigma is not my type.

Question 4.
A guy you've just met shows up at your door with a bunch of flowers. How do you react?

A. I'd be surprised, obviously – but also happy and flattered.
B. There are creepy nutters everywhere. I'd slam the door in his face.
C. If only! How come that only happens in commercials? I'd love a guy like that!

Question 5.
How would you describe your ideal guy?

A. Sporty and athletic.
B. Interesting and romantic.
C. Rich, generous and handsome.

Question 6.
If the setting was right, which of the following would be your preferred place to make love?

A. On a secluded beach in the moonlight.
B. In a comfortable and romantic setting, most likely at home.
C. Under the covers with the lights off.

Question 7.
Do you tend to postpone things?

A. I must admit that I do – especially chores and boring tasks.
B. Yes! I'm always late with everything.
C. No, not really. I'm pretty structured.

Question 8.
You're set on seducing a guy. What's your trick?

A. Emphasizing my feminine side.
B. I don't like seducing men.
C. Putting on a sassy outfit.

Question 9.
Do you like to keep yourself up-to-date with what's going on in the world?

A. Absolutely. I know everything there is to know about celebrities.
B. I'm about average, I guess. I watch the news and read newspapers most days.
C. Yes, I enjoy keeping myself informed. I love in depth stories

Question 10.
Would you describe yourself as emotional?

A. I'm romantic and sensitive, but not really emotional.
B. Yes, I can be, especially if someone hurts my feelings.
C. No. I don't get emotional. If I'm upset I put my foot down right away.

SCORE	A	B	C
Question 1	10	1	5
Question 2	1	10	5
Question 3	5	10	1
Question 4	5	1	10
Question 5	1	10	5
Question 6	10	5	1
Question 7	1	5	10
Question 8	10	1	5
Question 9	1	5	10
Question 10	10	1	5

75 – 100

Whatever you guys are doing, keep on doing it – it works! You don't even have to think about it; harmony just happens. You're finely tuned to each other's needs, and it's easy to make adventures happen. You share the same values when it comes to freedom, beauty, justice and sensuality. You are open-minded and flexible, and you would never betray each other's trust. This is a great match. Enjoy life – and each other.

51 – 74

Finally, you have met a man who has the ability to make you feel happy and loved, broaden your horizons, expand your vision and dreams and enlighten your spiritual self ... so don't mess up! Sure, his mind does seem to drift off every now and then, but this might even appeal to you. He is always searching, appreciating what's around him – and living. People pay thousands to attend seminars to make them mindful and in tune with the moment. This guy doesn't need that. His life is made up of individual moments – and maybe this is why he makes you feel so alive. Right now, you're here, enjoying the moment. The two of you have found something special. If you make an effort, it will continue to grow.

26 – 50

Well ... he may be a treasure, or he may be a pain. This depends on your values, your expectations and your attitude. You probably wish there was a bit more action and a little less talk. A bit more strength and masculinity; a little less poetry by candlelight. His sensitivity attracts you, but you long for a man who has his feet on the ground. Maybe you fell for this guy because of his interest in you – but that interest will shift easily to someone else unless you can manage to hold onto it. Love should flow freely. This one is up to you, really: you could make an effort and see how it goes, or you could look for someone who makes you feel love more effortlessly.

10 – 25

Let's be blunt about this. A once-off encounter could be fun. Anything beyond that will be a challenge – a big challenge. You have completely different outlooks on life. Your expectations are different. Your attitudes towards masculinity are different. But you won't have to worry about making a decision for the two of you. If things are not running smoothly, Mr Libra will move on without any trace of drama. Your ideal partner – and true happiness – is waiting somewhere else.

Thoughts...
Are you taking on a challenge for the right reasons? Are you seeing him, or are you seeing that man you wish he were? Happiness is precious. Embrace it - either with or without him. However, never leave without giving love a chance.

THE FEMALE

YOUR DATE: LIBRA
23 September–22 October

The Essence of her

Charming – good leader and organiser – tries to please everyone and can spread herself too thin – fair and impartial – positive and constructive – intelligent – diplomatic and cooperative – values harmony, beauty and balance – forthcoming – social – charming – eloquent – feminine, sensual and erotically creative, with a passionate streak – idealistic – big-hearted – compassionate

...and remember: Never underestimate a Libra. Although she may come across as innocently flirty, this is a sharp and intelligent woman. Pay attention to her.

Blind Date – speedy essentials

Who's waiting for you?

You should be waiting for her, not the other way around. She will probably capture your attention as soon as she walks through the door. She will look beautiful and perfectly put-together: hair, makeup, outfit – and smile. Even though her clothes may be a little revealing, there's something graceful about her. She is the kind of woman who can wear a seductive outfit and still look dignified. She is aware of her beauty and the effect she has on men, and this often creates an extra sparkle in her eyes. Her manner is warm, friendly and sensual, and that usually sets the tone for the evening...

Emergency fixes for embarrassing pauses.

It's very unlikely there will be any gaps in conversation. If she likes you, she will get the dialogue going. If she feels the whole thing was a mistake, she'll be off. Even if that's the case, she may rattle on with you for a while before making an excuse. She loves interacting with people. It gives her energy and inspires her.

Your place or mine?

Either – or whichever is closest. The Libra woman is open to erotic adventures, provided that a few things are right: the mood, the setting ... and the man. She is no pushover. It may take quite a while to seduce her on the first date. She must somehow feel confident that the guy will live up to her expectations. She loves the way a fling can add spice and excitement to her life, but deep down, she is secretly hoping that this man is the man

Checklist, before you dash out to meet her:

Wear a unique accessory

(hint: Show your eye for detail)

Check that your appearance is mirror-approved

(hint: Be well-groomed and attractive)

Have ideas for a surprise date suggestion

(hint: Make it intimate)

Make sure your flat is tidy, with refreshments in the fridge

(hint: In case she joins you there)

Avoid having early work the next morning

(hint: In case she stays)

Tip: Too much of a good thing is … well, too much. Balance and harmony are the essence of her life, and that applies to everything from work to love to sex.

CHAPTER 1

PREPARE YOURSELF

Catch her eye, capture her attention
Top 10 attention grabbers

1. Avoid macho moves; she prefers relaxed masculinity.
2. Admire and flatter her -- but avoid clichés. Be genuine and intelligent.
3. Tell her something unusual about yourself: an interest or a unique approach to life.
4. Show consideration for others.
5. Use a sensual voice and maintain a warm smile.
6. Items of luxury: a nice car, a watch etc.
7. Give her discreet and seductive glances.
8. Tell her about an artistic streak, whether that's a good voice, playing an instrument or being a photographer.
9. Know a thing or two about food and drink, but don't show off.
10. Be assertive – in general.

The HE. The man!

The Libra woman is looking for a man who can bring love, sensuality and balance to her life. Men often don't live up to her expectations, which is why she finds herself drifting from one to another. But it's not just the quest for her ideal mate that drives her. She is fond of men in general and loves being around them. Her friendly and playful attitude makes her very popular, and it takes a special man to pull her away from all the attention.

The Essence of him

Handsome – fit – interesting and intelligent – successful, or aspiring to be – drawn to the finer things in life – appreciates aesthetics, with an eye for beauty – generous– strong and protective – respects her need for freedom – inspiring – supportive – sensual, passionate and creative in bed – open-minded – social and friendly

---

Libra arousal meter
From 0 to 100... In 30 minutes. The setting needs to be right, and that includes her mood. It's important to take it slow and build the passion gradually.

Remember: Be true to yourself

It doesn't matter if she is the most stunning girl you've ever met – if you don't match, you don't match. You may be able to put on a show for a while to hold her attention, but what's the point? We can't please everybody. We all have different needs, dreams, tastes and preferences. There's no such thing as a one-size-fits-all lover. Be yourself, and be true to who you are – always!

Very important: Never push the Libra woman into anything. Give her time to make up her mind, or try persuading her gently by whispering in her ear. Be playful about it.

CHAPTER 2

THE FIRST DATE

Getting your foot in the door
The basics

No surprise visits. Thinking about popping by without advance warning? Forget it. She would hate for you to see her if she were looking scruffy.

High standards. Her outfit, makeup, hairstyle – and partner... everything needs to go well together. A date who looks like a mess won't stand a chance. A slightly dirty shirt? Don't think she won't notice - she will! In fact, the female Libra will notice details that other women would miss.

Style! She wants her partner to be as glamorous as she is – and preferably even more. If you can't afford to splash out on designer suits, at least look as though you have tried to make an effort: a nice, clean shirt, clean shave or a well-kept beard and freshly polished shoes will usually do the trick.

Artistic, sensitive - and strong! If you are a poet in disguise, let her know. She will sit down next to you and listen quietly while you recite your poems. However, sensitivity alone won't do it. She is fond of strength and masculinity. A strong body and muscular arms to hold her tight, will make her knees go wobbly.

Whatever you do...

• **DON'T** be cheap when you take her out.

• **DON'T** offer constructive criticism, if you've just met.

• **DON'T** make silly or crude jokes – and never on her behalf.

• **DON'T** keep her waiting for you to call, text or set up a date.

• **DON'T** give her fashion advice – unless you're a stylist.

Remember,
Even if you have managed to spark her interest, holding onto her is no easy task.

- **DON'T** be too relaxed about your looks. You won't get a second

chance.

- **DON'T** talk about previous girlfriends.

- **DON'T** forget about her if you bump into people you know.

- **DON'T** underestimate her. She is smarter than you think.

- **DON'T** neglect your manners or use foul language.

Show her your masculinity and sensitive sides – and be attentive to her.

Signs you're in - or not

If you're smart and good-looking, winning her over doesn't have to be a challenge. She will often take the initiative when a man has sparked her interest. The more fascinating she finds him, the more intense her approach. She doesn't mind using her body to signal her interest. She may even dress quite seductively – but her clothes will never be cheap and tacky. If she suspects she's found the man she's been looking for, she will use every trick in the book. Still not sure if she's really interested in you? Keep an eye out for the following clues:

Chances are she will...

- be very assertive, but in a non-aggressive way
- use her sensuality to tease you
- send you short and seductive text messages
- take an interest in what you are doing
- try her best to make you proud when you're out together; act gracefully, look stunning, etc
- surprise you with an unusual gift

Not your type? Making an exit

Although the Libra woman tends to move from one partner to another, don't mistake her for a romantic drifter. She is simply looking for her dream partner, but it's no easy task. He must strike a balance of being strong and masculine while also sensitive to beauty. He must be good-looking, but not spend every evening at the gym. She may have previously thought she'd met her mate, only to discover later that he couldn't live up to her expectations. It's quite simple, really: if you're not on her level, the balance will tip, and she'll be off.

There are always exceptions. You may have met a Libra who's intensely attracted to you, who feels a harmony with you and is convinced you're the man – but if you're convinced that you're not – it may be time to dish up a dose of reality.

Foolproof exit measures:

These options will be as much a challenge for you as they will be a shock for her. Be prepared to make yourself look bad...

- Be dull and boring
- Stop paying attention to your looks ... and hygiene
- Get nosy and inquisitive about her private life
- Criticize her clothes and tell her to dress more conservatively
- Insist on keeping sex quick and sweaty, and preferably in the morning
- Ditch your manners when you're at a restaurant
- Constantly compare her to others and say you wish she was different

CHAPTER 3

SEX'N STUFF

Seductive moves:
How to get her in the mood:

Although the Libra woman is sensual and easily turned on, she is just as easily turned off. In other words, never take anything for granted. Sassy suggestions are welcome, but make sure to avoid anything crude. Feel free to surprise her, but be sensual about it. Remember, sex with her is not confined to the bedroom. Use your imagination.

Preferences and erotic nature

Flattery and admiration are the key to everything with this woman, including sex. She responds quickly to positive attention, provided the man is classy and smart. A catcall from a scruffy stranger will elicit nothing but an icy stare. Still, she sometimes gets these, because this feminine woman can be a bit of an exhibitionist – although in a subtle way. She enjoys wearing clothes that show off the curves underneath – and sometimes a little more than she intended – but she manages to do so in a classy way. She enjoys casually seducing her partner by pottering around the house in revealing clothing. She may pretend she doesn't have sex on her mind, but she knows what she's doing. Miss Libra is a sensual firework.

Hitting the right buttons

Although every sign has areas on the body that are more sensitive than others, individual sensitivity may vary quite a bit. Don't go body-blind. Honing in on these erogenous zones and forgetting the rest of her is not a good idea. Use these areas to create sparks while turning her on, and as a passion-booster when things get heated. Watch her body language – including the most obvious of signs. Open your mind to the sensuality of touch and taste.

Key areas
Her hips and buttocks

Get it on
She would probably make a good samba dancer. Moving her derrière softly and sensually comes natural to her. Many female Libras enjoy dressing to emphasize their tush. If you add the hips, you have a substantial area that's very sensitive to touch, especially a light and playful touch...

Arouse her
You can stimulate her erogenous zones in many ways, even when the two of you are out in public. For instance, you might gently caress her buttocks while your arm is draped around her waist – or carefully rub your body against her while standing in a queue. The possibilities are endless. In bed, gentle bites and a light touch of your tongue in these areas will ignite her into a firework of passion.

Surprise her

Be a little old-fashioned to keep her on her toes. Buy her a bunch of flowers or a little gift you know she'll appreciate. Although this may come across as a simply romantic gesture, her appreciation may turn sensual as soon as she gets the chance.

Spice it up

A nice massage with warm oil over her hips and buttocks will make her tingle. Use enough oil to allow your hands – or your body – glide freely over her.

Remember: She has a liberal streak and may be more adventurous than she makes herself out to be. Her flare for exhibitionism can make things interesting...

Her expectations

Take it slow. Whatever you do, never rush her. She needs to set her own pace in order to thoroughly enjoy physical encounters. Any attempt to push her into the mood for sex will only turn her off.

Ease into it. Spending a long time on foreplay is very important to her, and it should always consist of both physical and mental stimulation.

Seductive and vocal. This woman loves having sweet nothings whispered into her ear while her partner is caressing her body.

Fresh and frisky. She belongs to one of the star signs that gets a kick out of having sex in the shower. Not only does it feel good, but it gives her and her partner a chance to freshen up before taking the event to the bedroom.

No aerobics, thank you! In the Libra woman's opinion, sex should be an aesthetic experience, not a sweaty waste of time.

Show your - creative - stuff. She appreciates an inventive partner, especially if he manages to combine sensual adventures with passionate admiration.

Your sensual preferences
Quiz yourself and find out whether this woman is for you.

Where on the scale are you?
1 = Don't agree | 3 = Sure | 5 = Agree!

1. Foreplay is important. It creates intimacy and helps build passion naturally.
One a scale for 1 to 5, you are: 1 - 2 - 3- 4 - 5

2. Sex doesn't have to be confined to the bedroom, or even to the indoors...
One a scale for 1 to 5, you are: 1 - 2 - 3- 4 - 5

3. I enjoy a sensual and liberated woman who can add new dimensions to sex.
One a scale for 1 to 5, you are: 1 - 2 - 3- 4 - 5

4. Verbal communication during sex can be arousing.
One a scale for 1 to 5, you are: 1 - 2 - 3- 4 - 5

Score.
15 - 20: Sensuality, intuition and intense pleasure combine to make this relationship hot.
14–10: You will probably enter through new erotic portals with this woman and experience sex in a more sensual way.
9–5: Remember, she will notice if you start taking it easy – either when it comes to looks or sensual attention. Want to make it work? Make an effort.
4–1: Hot and steamy, or romantic and sensual? You may find yourself debating your preferences. This connection could be fun and interesting, or it could be slow and boring.

CHAPTER 4

GENERAL STUFF

The big picture

Keep in mind that the characteristics of a Libra may vary quite a bit depending on where within the sign she was born, as well as a wide range of additional astrological factors. But for now, let's stick to the basics. Just remember: don't jump to conclusions as soon as you meet her. Give her room to shine. Get to know the woman behind the sign.

Her personality: Pros and cons

Pros
- Confident about her body
- Aesthetically inclined
- Feminine and friendly
- Artistic
- Harmonious
- Sexually creative
- Erotically intuitive
- Balanced
- Attractive
- Sensual
- Positive and optimistic
- Determined
- Conscientious
- Idealistic

Cons
- Exhibitionist
- A flirt
- A serial dater
- Narcissistic
- Stubborn
- Indecisive
- Superficial
- A drifter
- Afraid of criticism
- Confrontation-avoidant
- Restless
- Moody
- Spreads herself too thin
- Fickle

Tip: How to show romantic interest

You'll need to court, romance and woo the Libra woman in the old-fashioned way. Flowers, little gifts and lots of attention will go a long way. However, be careful not to come on too strong. Play it safe, and don't rush things.

Romantic Vibes

Miss Libra:
The romantic and loving partner

The essence

That special someone...   Although she's playful around men, she's idealistic about love and is always looking for that special partner who can fulfill her dreams. When she commits, her relationship needs be a source of inspiration.

No aggression, please. Arguments upset her. She would rather let things slide than get into a fight. She has the ability to see an issue from several sides, and this prevents her from jumping to conclusions.

Supportive. In order to avoid friction she needs to find a man who's on her level. As soon as she has committed to a relationship, she will be very supportive.

Keep it lively, keep it social. No matter whether she's in a relationship or not, she needs people around her.

Brighten up her spirits. She can get a little moody and restless, and a strong partner will be able to give her the strength and support she needs.

A true aesthetic. She wants a man who satisfies her need for beauty, both in his body and in his mind.

Tip: How to show erotic interest

Compliment her looks, and do it seductively. Comment on her curves, her hair and the way she carries herself. Make sure your voice is warm. Caress her with your words.

Erotic Vibrations

Miss Libra:
The aesthetic and liberated lover

The essence

Not just any setting... For romance to spark, the setting must be right. Scented candles and soppy music won't cut it. You'll need to take great care with your choice of music, wine and the atmosphere in general. A little extra attention will make a big difference.

Giving it all. She strives hard to achieve perfection, and this applies to her erotic life, as well.

Creative. She is creative and has a unique ability to turn the most traditional positions into something new and fun. Although she has some fixed ideas about sex, the Libra woman is a tolerant partner and is open to all sorts of suggestions.

Playful. She is often playful in her lovemaking. Don't be fooled into thinking that means she's inexperienced – it doesn't.

Frisky. She is a bit of an exhibitionist. She might want to arouse you by slowing stripping in front of you.

...and sensually confident. She has great confidence in her own sexuality, and she feels relaxed about it.

Make it beautiful. Be assertive in bed, but remember to be gentle, sensual and attentive. Make sex a beautiful experience.

CHAPTER 5

COMPATIBILITY QUIZ

Are you banging your head against the wall, or does she unleash your positive potential? Do you provoke her or bring out the best in her? Is she making you throw your arms into the air in exasperation, or do you feel inspired and complete in her company? Take the test to find out.

Question 1.
Do you feel appreciation for the beautiful aspects of life?

A. Absolutely. There is so much beauty in art, music and nature.
B. What beautiful aspects?
C. Sometimes, if I'm in the mood and not distracted.

Question 2.
Do you expect your partner to be explicit and assertive in bed?

A. Yes. Why should I always be the one to take charge?
B. Not at all. My partner gives me small hints, and that's good enough for me.
C. I expect her to participate actively, but nothing more.

(cont.)

Question no 3
Do you like a partner who is independent and takes care of herself?

A. Sure, but she doesn't have to be a high-flying career woman.
B. I just want her to be happy and follow her dreams. We'll support each other.
C. Yes! Then she can take care of me, too.

Question 4.
Do you ever tell your partner white lies in order to avoid conflict?

A. Yes. I hate arguments.
B. Seldom, and only very innocent ones.
C. Never. My partner is understanding, and I can discuss everything with her.

Question 5.
Do you think it's important to pursue separate interests while in a relationship?

A. Not just for the sake of it, but sure, if we have different interests.
B. No. What's the point of being in a relationship if we don't spend our time together?
C. Yes. By having separate experiences, we can grow as a couple.

Question 6.
Which of the following options would be your top choice for having sex?

A. On the beach in the moonlight.
B. In luxurious surroundings, with soft pillows and champagne.
C. In the backseat of my car.

Question no 7
Do you think it's important to romance your woman?

A. Absolutely! I'm old-fashioned when it comes to these things.
B. Not really, unless it's her birthday or a special occasion.
C. Sometimes, but it's easy to forget.

Question 8.
What does masculinity mean to you?

A. Being dominant and protective and taking care of my woman.
B. A strong mind in a strong body.
C. Being confident, and strong enough to show my sensitive side.

Question 9.
Would whispering erotic suggestions to your partner during sex be arousing for you?

A. A little. I usually do that when I'm already aroused.
B. Yes. It can add a new dimension to the experience.
C. Not really. It distracts me.

Question 10.
Are you particular about your appearance?

A. Not really, and I tend to forget to have my hair cut.
B. About average, I guess. I try to stay in shape and present myself well.
C. Absolutely. I enjoy looking good, and I have a keen eye for detail. I'm always well-groomed.

SCORE	A	B	C
Question 1	10	1	5
Question 2	1	10	5
Question 3	5	10	1
Question 4	1	5	10
Question 5	5	1	10
Question 6	10	5	1
Question 7	10	1	5
Question 8	1	5	10
Question 9	5	1	10
Question 10	1	5	10

75 – 100

Harmony, quality, excitement and intense erotic pleasure are only a few of the keywords that define this relationship – and things can stay this way, provided the two of you hold onto the feelings you are experiencing now. You share the same values and enthusiastic approach to life. You help her find her feet when her indecisiveness takes over, and she brightens your days with beauty and sensual surprises. You may be different in many areas of life, but you fulfill each other and create a rare and loving relationship.

51 – 74

The two of you have the ability to bring out the best in each other. This relationship is far too rewarding to be clouded with silly details. If problems arise, try communicating openly and gently. Never approach her with a problem and demand an opinion. Diplomacy is the key, and she'll be more than happy to discuss things with you if you choose a soft approach. Pay attention to her needs, both inside and outside the bedroom. If you're not sure how she feels about something, ask her. Never make her feel like you're taking her for granted. A nice compliment may not mean much to you, but it can make her feel incredibly good inside. Inspire her. Let both your masculine and sensitive sides shine. A strong, positive and sensual partner can make her feel relaxed and in-tune with the world.

26 – 50

You're probably feeling a little confused by this woman. What's on her mind? Where does she want to go in life? Chances are that she doesn't know herself. Sex may be fun, but it will take more than a few moments of passion to build a lasting relationship. The Libra woman can be very indecisive. She hates conflict and sometimes gets moody. Add these things together, and you have an enigma. You need to be direct with her, but try to avoid being blunt. If you're too strong, she'd rather agree than fight, and this will solve nothing. Take a constructive approach. Be attentive, positive and complimentary. Pamper her. If she still seems evasive, then it's probably time to look for happiness elsewhere.

10 – 25

Pulling your hair won't do it. You either need to become more constructive or admit that this adventure is coming to an end. You may be attracted to her for many reasons, but they may not be the right ones. Ultimately, she is probably far too evasive for you. One day she's super positive, and the next day she's not so sure. Her obsession with looks, both her own and yours, are probably driving you nuts. Is it really necessary to spend half an hour in the bathroom before nipping out to buy some milk? If you're running out of patience and not prepared to talk it all through, then this might be the end.

Thoughts...

Confused about the results in the quiz? Don't be. Only you know how you feel about this woman, and how much you are willing to work in order to make the relationship last. Be honest about your feelings and let them guide you.

...just a final note:
This book has not been approved by your date and should be treated accordingly. He or she *may* not agree with the content.

www.ingramcontent.com/pod-product-compliance
Lightning Source LLC
Chambersburg PA
CBHW071838020426
42331CB00007B/1776